Weapons for Massive Building

**WMB FOR EVERY BUSINESS
OR BECOME
A SITTING DUCK**

JP Rincon

Weapons for Massive Building.

Copyright© 2017

All Rights Reserved.

No part of this book may be used or reproduced in any manner whatsoever without written permission except in the case of brief quotations embodied in critical articles and reviews.

ISBN-13: 978-1974592661

ISBN-10: 1974592669.

CONTENTS

Introduction

Chapter 1. The Tank

Chapter 2. The Rocket Missiles

Chapter 3. The V.I.P Badge

Chapter 4. The Measuring Tape

Chapter 5. The Emergency Kit

Chapter 6. The Samurai Machete

Chapter 7. The Oxygen Mask

Chapter 8. The Knight's Vision Goggles

Chapter 9. The Smart Phone

Chapter 10. The Stop Watch

Chapter 11. The Chivalry Flag

Chapter 12. The Key Chain

Chapter 13. The Expandable Business Card

Chapter 14. The Cookie Cutter

Chapter 15. The Sphere Magnet

Chapter 16. The Mirror

Chapter 17. The Global Positioning System

Chapter 18. The Goody Bag

Chapter 19. The Thank You Card

Dedication

Introduction

It is always fun to skip stones on perfectly still water and watch the ripples. Almost all youngsters try it at least a few times just because it comes naturally. It is much like a sport since it requires a technique and a goal to challenge a set of standards. A game where engineers and like-minded people face the yield of the following two forces:
1. Matter (Flat surface on a rock spinning on its axis forcing a direction) and
2. Chemistry (measure density, speed and angle to keep rock afloat).

Once you find the right equation it becomes euphoric! With practice you will get more ripples and you master the game. Just like the real secret in business, which is to never let go of that kid inside of you, and to never forget how to enjoy the moment. That curious inner child in all of us, loves challenging games and everyone should take that happy kid out more often.

Owning a business might be easier than you think because it is in essence a game. It has a set of rules, you use your imagination, you use your best winning strategy and then you set yourself up for the big win. Let's take for example a trained Navy Seal. He or she must be equipped and trained, in every possible way, with the most sophisticated technological systems to be the most efficient of the warriors and survive under harsh environments. If a Navy Seal is placed in the middle of the Amazon's forest at midnight without moon light, it should be a walk in the park for the Seal using his or her advanced tools and methods to anticipate every situation. The Seal knows he or she can use rainwater for many things in order to survive, and which poisonous frogs to hunt and how to stay at the top of the food chain.

The real warrior is trained in Aikido Martial Arts techniques; he or she use the opponents force and energy to create momentum and used it for your good protecting you while using the least amount of energy.

The same goes for the real entrepreneur at heart. He or she is always prepared to push the boundaries of the known into the unknown. It is a magical weapon if you conquer such a virtue. It is to get comfortable with the uncomfortable to find the right equation because it keeps you moving just like any other living organism.

Most business owners tend to see the good side because of their natural tendency of being creators and dreamers. It is nice to think that all stories will end with a happily ever after. However, first you need to survive the climax part of the story. You can have your happily ever after if you incorporate all the magical weapons mentioned in this book. Otherwise, you will face gravity or worse; flatline. The reason why so many companies have closed their doors and failed. Many smart professionals can sense the company's structure is weak and they leave before it collapses. I was one of those fortunate professional travelers, moving from industry to industry to another industry again. I now say "fortunate" because it made me a stronger entrepreneur.

At first, it might not sound like the best idea changing from industry to industry and starting from the bottom of the ladder many times, but it paid the bills while I was going to college, plus the experience I received was priceless. Then, I got to understand clearly what my strengths and weaknesses are. I now enjoy every second of each new job, accepting every experience humbly. I also made a lot of mistakes but that is a way of learning too. Sometimes you need to experience water to know what is wet. As a result, my passion and knowledge for growing businesses increased exponentially. I also had many managerial positions and I had opportunities to study and question everything even when I was not asked to do so.

Also, growing up with a family involved in the private sector was a gift. My parents, grand-parents, all my aunts and uncles had private businesses but only did average. I came to the U.S. when I was 17 years old by myself, looking to get ahead in life, just like all the great ancestors of this nation that pursued that freedom and happiness. It is indeed a journey to pursue your dreams since they are not given to you by nature. It is a great learning curve following a great line, "do the best you can with what you have". I recognize now that I am older, I didn't do very well at first with people but I didn't get intimidated by those experiences. I understood later that was a clash of cultures and also ignorance on my part. Embracing those experiences instead was the only way for me to move forward in life.

Especially because I was away from my family, in a completely different country, speaking a different language, and living with different customs. The survival and ingenuity mechanisms within my own soul helped me stay attentive, ask questions, and I did not content myself with the first answer I received either. I had to experience those questions, and put them into practice since I had no other choice. The worse you can do is to conform yourself with the first answer. After a few trail and errors, I transformed a few of those experiences into metaphysical tools for entrepreneurs to achieve goals and keep focus on winning. These tools also called "Weapons for Massive Building" are the ones I am about to share with you.

I have had the privilege of working very closely over 60 different industries, all across the ladder. Every position you can think of, I was there learning and teaching. When you are curious and have worked in many industries, you will understand a thing or two: First, no matter how big your company is, at the end of the day we all sell a commodity, which is a benefit. There is a need to increase value all the time.

Second, if you are not increasing those benefits then you are not in business, or soon will not be. That means you are flatlining, and need to try new ideas to improve revenue. We are in the age of information and the competition moves very fast. These Weapons for Massive Building, or WMB are paying off in my life, and now it's time for me share my experiences with everyone.

These WMB are made to sharpen your skills and senses for the concrete jungle environment of the business world. Plus, they will empower you as a real warrior moving you forward regardless of the circumstance. WMB's will invite you to take a look within your organization to discover areas of improvement. At the end of this book you will be ready to install every WMB into your subconscious and they become second nature. The WMB will help you think strategically and help you see your business with a different set of eyes with a 20/20 view. In return, it will give you new ideas on how to embrace different situations to set you up for success. Similar to going to the gym, you will add muscle to your business, therefore, giving you a greater advantage over your competitors. This means real change will start taking place as soon as you finish this book.

You will have a beautiful well rounded and peaceful business. Once you start using the WMB on a regular basis, people will start saying that you are a lucky person. However, you will respond that luck for you is readiness meeting opportunity. The secret here is to know what is valuable enough to wait patiently for and to obtain it at the right moment.

Just like the successful equation of the saying "the early bird catches the worm". The bird is obedient to that present law and respects its timing, so the smart bird makes priority for this special time. He should be ready! It also goes hand in hand with the saying, "timing is everything", you need to be ready for when the time comes.

The trick is to learn from history since history always repeats itself; therefore you know what is coming, so you can predict the future this way. Some call themselves prophets but they are just people paying attention. Also, it is healthy to keep Murphy's Law in mind. Everything could go wrong in any given situation, if you give it a chance.

The Universe will be in charge of filling in the gaps that are required to be learned by nature...the only organic way: cause and effect. Everything is an equation and by law it is a balanced statement. The same way WMB will give you the guidance and preparedness to overcome any circumstances by understanding your surroundings, and giving you a greater sense of awareness. Once you use them on a daily basis, you will find joy doing businesses. Effective systems will follow once you are truly providing real benefits.

Another key factor within your industry is education. Finding ways to improve your thinking at all times, it is just like finding the true North within ourselves. You will not get real education from just one book, or just one institution, nor in your peers, nor friends.

It is an individual's journey that can take the seed, plant it and harvest it into a huge tree. It is those life experiences that will teach you to focus on what is important to your future and how to make the most out of your gifted skills as a business owner.

It is important to write down your experiences, positive and most important negative ones, so keep a journal. Write everything down because the more information you have the more you will remember. 'There is no learning without remembering' said Socrates. It will help you go back in time and meditate on situations that make you weak and those that make you stronger and re-use those ideas. Feed yourself from that energy if you know how to channel it.

Most business owners are too busy trying to solve all the problems themselves which is being in reaction mode. Einstein once said "the intelligence that got you in that problem will not have the capacity to get you out". In other words, you need to be outside the cathedral bell when you are ringing it, not in it. You will need the help of an outsider to help you open that door. Someone that can slip you the key from under the door. Most industries use only one or two methods that someone two generations ago considered outside the box. It is time for you to be that game changer.
Therefore my warrior friend, buckle-up for this great journey of your business game, and the Weapons of Massive Building that will help you withstand any weather and circumstance.

"The way to get started is to quit talking and begin doing." -Walt Disney

The Tank

Chapter 1

The amazing armored tank is one of the most technological and accurate weapons used through history. Originally inspired by Leonardo DaVinci's, a circular tank designed with canons all around to cover every possible angle of attack with purpose to control certain areas. Nowadays we see them in all sizes and shapes. Big, small, amphibian-like, and others just plain fast on the ground. There are many different types of tanks for different tasks; some have green camouflage loaded with rocket launching missiles with two iron track belts as wheels that can withstand heavy artillery. Others are like the Batman tank that is fast, accurate and that carries a bike inside the tank to change when needed.

As a business owner you need to see your company as a Tank of war. The components of the Tank is what is the moving force of the company. Propelled by the will of the mission statement and all the experiences in between since day one.

Every year something new needs to be added to the Tank, so make sure that what you are keeping is worth carrying. Don't be a hoarder and carry things that will make you heavy and not flexible.

Another feature in the tank is that some are equipped with 360 degree cameras that zoom and can see upcoming challenging scenarios from very far away. Also, when giving directions there is a Left and Right, not a Left and Wrong, just like driving your business. The gas pedal is geared by the hard step of the will in the mission of the company and those principles/values is the fuel combustion inside those pistons. The Mission Statement has to be written from the heart with values that will inspire all warriors inside the Tank.

These inspired warriors will then model the continuation of such principles, thickening the outside metal of the Tank. These great metal walls will keep out the artillery sent by the competition. It is okay to call it friendly fire here because it is very healthy to compete with other great players.

Keep growing until your Tank is so big that it will dwarf any competition. The real winning plan is to dominate that market with your Tank. To move forward we observe that the front set of gears are moving forward and bringing the caterpillar tracks/belts towards the back. The gears move forward by inspiration of past experiences, where as a result of this comes maturity. That special and courageous gift of maturity will give the Tank more torque, so the gears and the caterpillar tracks can keep moving without any problem.

Every bolt and nut is what keeps the tank together, and in the same way, the infrastructure of the Tank must be solidified or embedded to make it indestructible. It can be small as a one person or as large as a cruise ship. Let values, principles, benefit and respect remain the same.

These beliefs are the walls being shaped as impenetrable armour shields. Then, undoubtedly, the tank will always be ready for action because it is equipped to confront any situation. If you are not prepared, then your tank becomes just a delivery van with all your tools trapped in taped up, and unmarked boxes. You will be in reaction and not in control. Just to be clear, it is very important to understand that before you can power on the Tank, you need to be a trained blind folded warrior. Knowing exactly where the steering wheel, gas pedal, brake pedal, and gears are to stay on the right path for a safe journey. A legendary warrior will master each of his or her Katanas or weapons of choice. All real legendary warrior tools are made for precise situations with the intention to protect the Tank and to create an honest community.

When exercised properly, the faith within the company keeps everything solidified and as a result all warriors inside the Tank will be inspired to perform better, making them stronger. Consequently, your Tank becomes brighter within that industry, illuminating your path, and allowing others to follow; rising straight to the top.

Solid.

Ohm's Law: $V = I \times R$

"It does not matter how slowly you go so long as you do not stop." -Confucius

The Rocket Missiles

Chapter 2

Once you have a clear target, fire away! Ideas are the greatest assets you can possibly own, and you already do it! Sadly, most of those ideas never get launched because of fear or they are simply overlooked. I state most of the times it is fear because business owners are busy and fear something could go wrong or they are afraid of wasting time on the unknown.

Also, understanding what not to do is half the answer. Trying new ideas is a win-win situation even when at first it seems like you lost money and/or time. I call this 'finding the right equation' since I get smarter every time I send a Rocket Missile to understand my targets. This is the #1 tool inside the Tank and it is the most important tool for survival. It is used to attain any goal you want when you know how to use it. Some missiles ideas are so powerful, that they literally go out of this world.

The Rocket Missiles ideas are breakthroughs by someone really curious. That is what we all are striving to obtain unanswered questions to complete the equation. There is a great saying, shoot for the moon, even if you miss, you still land among the stars.

The most important part of this missile idea is to have a GPS tracker to know exactly where the missile is headed or it will orbit around the planet. You don't need to be a rocket scientist to understand your market nor to listen to it's pulse. Missile ideas will give you the answer, just like a probe, showing you what is hot and what is not; if you really pay attention where the rockets land.

The most important step is the final one. Record all launches evaluations and conclusions so you don't waste time or money. As a result, your Tank will move you ahead of the game systematically and exponentially. Once you observe where the missile ideas are dropped, you will move accordingly as you see the results. You will then direct the cannon either towards the East, the West, the North, or the South. Those coordinates will have to make sense just like any mathematical equation for them to match and work like a charm.

It is very important to orchestrate all systems at the same time while sending rocket missiles. It might sound a lot but if you are a business owner, then I am confident to say that you have it in your blood. Just be ready to have all WMB in place while sending rocket missiles for an everlasting effect.

Don't be afraid to launch "blank" rocket missiles, they are completely healthy for the company as well. These are try out missiles that will guide you for the real ones and the big ones too. It is already a familiar area or tested territory, telling you something about the path to take. This way the Tank can be directed towards the safest and fastest way possible. For example Thomas Edison made 10,000 ways of how not to make an incandescent bulb according to him. An idea and the courage to follow it through is what makes the difference in adding benefits for clients to come back.

Fortune favors the bold, so keep launching ideas. Try to find as many ways to improve your Tank as possible, so try a "Blank" Missile for your next launch. The only and best way to find great results is to test them. It is literally a science. So when you do find the right equations inside the Tank, you will be creating a WMB with missile ideas. Therefore when you launch them, they will be the biggest and brightest fireworks in the night sky; giving you a broader exposure, and taking over the competition in your area.

Also, a rocket missile could split a mountain in two for the Tank to move along through it. The reality is that to be a great launcher of missile ideas it requires a few virtues. The first is courage to take you to the next step. Be confident. Second is to be fearless, you will have to empty the cup of knowledge and let other experiences lead you. Unlearn. It's okay to fail. Third is clarity: You will need to have clear thoughts and a well written mission statement so you know exactly what your mission is about and what your position is. Fourth is trust. It is required to have a tranquil mind to let these missiles navigate by themselves with the least resistance possible. Last but not least, be positive. When you are happy and find yourself with a positive entourage, you will find it very easy to find more solutions than when stressed and bullied.

Go ahead and send a few missiles a day, and don't forget to record all benefits added to your

Tank. Once you find the right coordinates to this equation, in other words you hit bulls-eye, then multiply each method used.

Imagine.

<u>Newton's Second Law of Motion: $F = M \times A$</u>

"When you aim for perfection, you discover it's a moving target." -Unknown

The V.I.P Badge

Chapter 3

It is also known as the rank or title within a division. Just like it is used in the military, it gives a quick reference guide of the chain of command to follow. It is an accurate delegation system thanks to the understanding of the accountability process of the organizational chart. It will reveal to those who use this tool how strong the infrastructure of their company is. It shows if they are running smoothly or in reaction.

Your organizational chart will determine the process and each role's accountability. If you do not have an organizational chart with roles and processes, then please make one now. It doesn't matter how small your company might be, it is a must to give a title to each important ramification of the company. Once successful, you will be asked to increase your army of warriors as necessary. Now you will be ready to accommodate such demand easily.

All managers and team leaders must be accountable for their work and their performance. Like with heavy machinery, if the brakes or steering system malfunction it affects everything and the machine simply stops working. We cannot blame the steering system for the brakes not working, etc. All employees should perform only one task at the time, this way it easier to measure performance and it gives you an upper hand in the situation, giving you. I believe the human mind is very unique and it is expandable when asked for hard tasks, especially when survival is at hand. However, I believe the employee should have one rank and one task as an objective: become a master in a short period of time. I believe that when employees have two or three titles. The quality of their work is diluted exponentially. It is like calling and getting half an answer or no answer at all. Others believe that employees could get bored and deviate from work, so then, they ask the employee to wear another hat while they are in flight or fight stage. Which means to me that they are facing an emergency landing or most likely a possible crash.

The average employee wants to always do right but will deviate if systems are not in place with positive reinforcements. So, if the employee has some down time, invite them into the game of making the area of their work better by rewarding them in other areas that won't cost much for the business. Even if it cost you something, at the end of the day it is far less expensive than not knowing the potential in your company. To improve the area means to thicken the metal in your tank.

Once everyone does it according to the warrior's orchestration, you will end up with a Tank made out of gold; stronger and brighter than ever. You must invest time observing each area and how to improve to get to the next level of greatness. The organizational chart is the first thing the warrior must do. He needs to see the end result as a clear and definite outcome for each of his very important team mates.

Just to be clear and to draw the line here in delegation process and responsibilities, the steering wheel can only be given to the driver, no questions asked. The steering wheel cannot be passed around. Two people steering is even worse. It also applies to the president over stepping experts' advice. It only makes sense to me to leave technical matters to the ones who have dedicated a great amount of time in that field. Each role individually appreciated can only evolve into a greater experience for the client, which in return will take care of the Tank.

Pyramid.

<u>All for one, and one for all: 1=0.99999</u>

"When the student is ready, the Master appears."

– Buddhist Proverb

The Measuring Tape

Chapter 4

This is by far one of my favorite WMB to use almost in most any situation you can encounter. It is a very necessary tool since it will give you precision and guidance. You must measure your body to get the perfect size to fit you, right? Since you know your measurements, you get the best that fits you. If you do not know your size, then things will be too loose or too tight. Not paying attention to those details will make you look like a clown, one that trips over his long pants and big shoes. Inside the warrior's journey there will be many situations that will require different methods of measuring something, just like in construction, measure twice and cut once. Measurements can be taken in different ways like for example just by looking at the company records or by giving out surveys to clients. Either way you will have to embrace mathematics since in business it is a story being told only with numbers.

Not the complicated math, although you can really get complicated if you want, but the point is to know what you are adding, multiplying, or subtracting. You cannot put anything to the test unless you know the primary statistics. This reminds me that common sense must be applied, otherwise it would be nonsense. Get in the habit of weighing experiences. Track each step of the way and file them away. Record the bad as well so you don't make the same mistake later. I have to be clear about the following, only use the ones with a positive result. Even if they are not your first choice, the results show you the better product.

Measuring is like the "you are here" on a map. This way you know how much distance you need to travel from where you are and if your tank will fit down those avenues. I will be honest with you, measuring is not an easy task at first but once you notice it works just like the odometer on your car, you would need to follow speed limits for your protection. In that same way, you will see when the company is adding those benefits and bingo! That is where the honey springs up to make your life sweeter. It really is nice to meet other ways of measuring everything inside your own business.

An example for measuring is if you spend X amount of dollars on a banner, in the middle of Time Square NY. How many calls did you get from that ad? What happens when you change a small word or two? How many prospects as a result? X is the baseline and the inviting words (copyright) are the variables. If you are not measuring these methods and systems, you are in reaction my friend warrior. You need to get the Tank cranking in a different gear to move it far from that quick sand. Your money will be swallowed quickly if you don't pay attention.

Simply by asking questions is the only way to get the real sense of experience from the client. That is really when it becomes a personal or customized experience making your prospect into a lifetime client. In other words, you are asking your client to fire at your Tank to make sure all your walls are capable to withstand their pressure. Once you know such measurements by heart, then you will be like an Olympian running and jumping the obstacles. Making it look all super easy.

Get this, this is just one field plane, if you test in many areas of your business and start applying what is working, then you will be growing exponentially.

Fit.

<u>Quadratic Equation: $ax^2 + bx + c = 0$</u>

"Statistics suggest that when customers complain, business owners and managers ought to get excited about it. The complaining customer represents a huge opportunity for more business".

Zig Ziglar

Emergency Kit

Chapter 5

Ouch that hurts! As much as we do not want get hurt sometimes it happens. We are curious living beings, especially when we start learning something new in life. We have to move through the adolescence stage quickly because falling off the bike is hard.

Ignorance leads to pain but perfection follows practice. Just like the coordination of balancing the body on two legs and sometimes on one leg while you are moving the other leg. Babies will just keep trying until they start running first, then take it easy and walk. In the meantime, as a warrior, you need to be prepared at all times for the worst scenario, so let's get real. If you create a cushion on the floor it is easier on your body, when you fall right? The same principle goes for the Tank.

Preparation is key for survival since it is a bumpy road in the beginning with unprecedented tasks.

You will need the following items inside your own Emergency Kit:

1.An unopened box where you find instructions to plan B and Plan C. These must be easy to understand. They are ideal at times of stress and emergency when our minds tend to block and shut down a few senses since survival mode just kicked-in.

2. Then you will find, MRE's boxes. These boxes stand for Money Reserved Especially. These boxes of MRE are cushions to cover certain situations. This is the #1 priority to survive in hard times. These are the eggs that are not in the other basket, if you know what I mean. These could be in liquid assets or IRA's resulting in an impenetrable shield around your tank.

The MRE need to be ready to be used when necessary and they need to be replaced when used, the sooner the better. On top of the MRE you will have the name of the person or company you choose ahead of time to solve issues like the one at hand solve ASAP. The name and contact information should appear handy in the front and sides of the packaging since it is the number you need to call. Just like dialing 911 for emergencies. If you have speed dial, then that is even better.

3. The next item will be a camera. It is necessary in every Emergency kit. When you have an accident usually you take the picture of the car, the license plate, insurance and registration of the person other party involved in the accident. The camera for a business is necessary to freeze for a moment all systems and back up a little so you can see the whole picture. What I mean is that most warriors are so busy that it is always healthy to take a step back and see where you need some improvement. Little details usually add value, just like the mint with the receipt at your favorite restaurant. Learn how to capture these moments and you will have a great album of photos to learn from.

4. The next item inside the Emergency Kit is a pair of clear glasses with ear plugs. It is a one-step action that will protect two of your
most necessary senses in business. By blocking the sound and blocking any distraction will help you focus and increase productivity within the other senses. Sometimes it could be loud inside the tank so you will need to proudly wear those ear plugs in times of focusing and delivering the goals. Once you do that you will strengthen your other senses, and then you can take on bigger challenges. Distractions inside the tank are venom and it can really carry things away from your goals. Keep these shields on and continue moving forward.

5. The next item is one that most people forget to use. Something that multiplies your good energy that helps you move forward when nothing else can. Pumping up your "jam' music" like Journey's, "Don't stop, believen' or 24K from Bruno Mars, whatever! You need all the pumping and cheering you can possibly get. If you are married and your partner is a cheerleader that is perfect because you will need to hear that encouragement on a regular basis. Also, you can also do it yourself with a mantra you need to incorporate into your subconscious. I personally encourage a combination of both. This is what feeds your soul and forces you to overcome any circumstance. There will be moments when you, the warrior, will feel defeated but the cheering and believing will help motivate you to get up and continue the game; learning and applying that knowledge.

6.Last but not least, you will need to have in the Emergency Kit a copy of this book. This book will help you understand the relationships between the tools with an easy message to remember. Each tool carries a deep meaning that can be used on a daily basis.

These emergency tools must be put to practice to sharpen your mind and help you as a business owner to determine the areas you need to improve to keep your tank moving forward.

Anticipate.

<u>Mass–Energy Equivalence: $E=mc^2$</u>

"Believe you can and you're halfway there." - *Theodore Roosevelt*

The Samurai Machete

Chapter 6

Monkey see, monkey do. We are not too far from the monkey's curiosity and their methods inside. In every industry we see trends that have worked for decades, so they stick to it and make it a norm. So a person with great experience in their field will only know one or two ways that are effective unless they ask questions outside that industry's infinity loop. People with these tendencies usually get ideas from competitors. You know from the get go those people are not effective. They are falling behind somebody else and they learn very little or nothing.

So it's like having a Samurai sword and using it like a machete to cut weeds, grass, bushes and hitting rocks and concrete to finish the work. It will take double the energy and time to prevail. The idea is for you to go directly to the source of your system and ask the guru to train you well in using these weapons for a successful fight.

The Samurai sword will then be used to its best capacity in a beautiful and coordinated way to perform within the challenges like a peaceful warrior, in harmony. The training part is the most important; practice makes perfect. The training will help you sharpen your movements and strengthen your control over your weapon of choice. To be able to do that you will need to empty your cup of knowledge. Sometimes we need to say, 'I do not know', in order to be able to grasp the most of what is being taught. In general, if you enter questioning, you will come out knowing. However, if you come in knowing you will come out questioning. This is the only way to deeply and honestly learn something new. You will not miss one movement because you will be in the moment at all times.

Once you have mastered a method, you can set cruise control with automatic sensors so you can move onto the next one. Compare your outputs, ideas, and then leverage to see which one makes more sense to use in your life. Bruce Lee said "I fear not the man who has practiced 10,000 kicks once, but I fear the man who has practiced one kick 10,000 times". The weapons you master are your best allies, since they will be the ones to deliver the answers to an easier life. Always choose to focus on building muscle for your skills, therefore, you will turn your machete into a beautiful samurai sword.

Enhance.

Photoelectric Effect Formula: $E = hf$

"If my mind can conceive it, and my heart can believe it, then I can achieve it." -Muhammad Ali

The Oxygen Mask

Chapter 7

Use your nose and breathe in as much air as possible, then let it go slowly through your mouth. This action alone gives you a more balanced mind set, and that is why this is one of the most important tools inside the tank. It is important to be mindful of your breathing at all times. In plain terms oxygen keeps us alive and in balance. When too much oxygen is taken in, it makes you dizzy, so you will need to know exactly how long to wear the mask.

Just like when we spend a few hours a day in a room, we get used to the smell but when we step out and come back, we experience difference again. It is the same for your company. You will need to take time off or even take a day or two off during the week. It will give you a win-win situation because two things will happen: One, your mind will be relaxed as well as your muscles. Two, your business systems will be tested to see if it will fly solo.

You will learn to trust and rely on your bullet proof tank and its systems to guide all your warriors. Your level of delegation and efficiency will be incremented; giving you more time to do what is important in your life. That is the sole purpose of the warrior to fight for his freedom.

By using the Oxygen mask you will have a more defined definition of relaxing and enjoying your life; it is everything but work! This is where the cup of knowledge really gets emptied out. Giving you a fresh start next time you step into the tank. For those who are really far from having an oxygen mask here is a list: Spend time with family, friends, exercise, read, travel, camp, ski, kayak, watch movies, dine out, volunteer, leisurely walks around the park, do yoga in front of a lake or ocean. So many activities are positive for your mind and spirit. I am sure you get the point of having an Oxygen mask inside your tank.

The result of not using this wonderful tool, will be like a wave not crashing at the shore and it just keeps going inside the streets, causing chaos. Or like a gas pipe getting hotter and hotter by the minute until it explodes. The Oxygen Mask tool is used by professionals in many ways and many times during the day. That little golf set at the office goes a long way. It gives you a mental and soulful variation with your everyday thinking. It disrupts the beating of the conversation and then you can start fresh again. Plus, you will be pumping blood and oxygen back into your brain because you are moving your body differently.

Using the Oxygen Mask is literally being in the moment enjoying what is at the eyes reach. It will activate all 5 senses for their maximum. It is called the present because it is a gift. Let's play with the present the best we can possibly imagine just to make a stronger come back. That is the reason successful business warriors love to do what they do and it is because they find leverage; giving them a more relaxed brain, and resulting in creation of ideas every minute of the day.

Bliss.

Jacobi's Method: Ax=b

"It is not the man who has too little, but the man who craves more, that is poor". –Seneca

WEAPONS FOR MASSIVE BUILDING

The Knight's Vision Goggles

Chapter 8

Back in the Middle Ages, a knight was a gentleman and a warrior trained to develop everything with perfect courage, wisdom, and compassion. Also known as Chivalry, which is a moral system along the rules of their constitution, also they exercise concepts of bravery, courtesy, justice, hope, love, and honor. These are the traits of a real warrior inspired by faith, fighting to protect the assets of the pledged empire. Knights are disciplined and they display their beliefs at all times; much like the way the business warrior should see his or her mission statement carried inside the Tank. When you wear the Knight's Vision Goggles, you will then see the terrain differently since you will be treating it with extra responsibility and respect. These Goggles will give you a vision like no other, you will see inside and outside of all systems. Only then, you will find the right substance to help leverage the movements within all systems.

The Knight's Vision Goggles will magnify situations coming at you from a distance. It will guide you to step away from quicksand fields. Once you wear these goggles you will get a sense of awareness, like binoculars in a watch tower. It is a moment to take a look within your industry and see how the domino effect is taking place, so your timing will be just right. Knights will travel, not only with torches at night to scare animals at times, but they also have the capability to travel in stealth mode. Like waiting for the next full moon to travel at night depending on the mission. When you anticipate you will always remain in control of the situation.

The Knight's Vision Goggles will have to be used on a regular basis since markets change rapidly. This is a very important point to remember. Sometimes technology, or a better way of doing something, comes along and then it becomes the new standard in your industry. For example, VHS was replaced fast by the DVD or the Beeper by the cell Phone.

The Knight's Vision Goggles tool will empower you to move your Tank forward in a safe zone because you have taken the time to look ahead of your path and know what is about to come to your way. This is why it's so important to have a profound mission statement, with the true North embedded in your book of operations to positively impact your goals. Hitting bulls-eye every time. Knights work to protect their nation and to improve all social aspects within their borders. Therefore, there is no room for being a crook, nor having the wrong intentions. Giving the Knights' ability to perform only the healthy deals.

Another way to use the Knight's Vision Goggles is to help you see the intangible assets within your business. Because Knights deal at a moral level, then it will be easier to find such intangibles and make them work towards your amortization. All you need to do is to look at the manual of instructions within your industry and find those elements that are worthy of your Tank and have them assessed by a professional.

Take for instance the Coca-Cola brand name, it is worth more than a billion dollars. When you show proof of such asset to banks, they will be glad to lend you money. It is a great way to accomplish your business goals. When you wear the Knight's Vision Goggles it's like not only understanding the ocean, but you can also make waves within your industry, and then surf on top of them because the ball will be in your in court. In addition, to get to this stage you need to ask a lot of questions, and preferably the uncomfortable ones.

For example, Colonel Sanders was a warrior that had to wear the Knight's Vision Goggles when a highway was constructed on top of his restaurant and he saw he was going out of business quickly. Colonel Sander's Tank moved to friendlier territory and took it to the next level by asking tough questions. He truly was a Knight warrior because he lived his life with an 'all or nothing' mentality, so he went big. You either go big or go home.
Just like Henry Ford said once, "Whether you think you can, or you think you can't
--you're right."

Another example of how to use the Knight's Vision Goggles is by studying your competitors with an X-Ray vision. The Knight's Vision Goggles will make you aware of how their infrastructure is composed. Take your time to meditate on their moves and find their flaws or weak spots. That will give you a clue, which will guide you to move in that direction to get a point up over your competitors. Most industries are "married" to a few methods used from generations ago because a brilliant person was thinking differently. Everyone looks up to who is doing great at the moment because that is the easiest route.

However, a true warrior knows he is the front leader like in a bird pack taking V formation: Strong enough to break the wind for the others.

Inspire.

Pythagoras' Theorem: $a2=b2+c2$

"I'm a great believer in luck, and I find the harder I work the more I have of it". -Thomas Jefferson

The Smart Phone

Chapter 9

We are all very much familiar with this WMB. In my opinion, we use our cell phones way too much. However, the smart phone is only smart when it dials the right number and at the right time. Otherwise, is a dumb phone. Just imagine how embarrassing it would be if by mistake the phone unlocks itself in your bag or pocket, and then dials your boss when you are making jokes at your friend's house... it's no joke.

The same happens when we dial the wrong number to our clients. Worse yet, answer with the wrong attitude or say disrespectful comments and your prospective client hangs up before you say another word. This is another precision tool to help you understand your contact list of clients. The contacts list will show you a picture and the ringtone for every contact. Can it get more clear than that?

It is a unique Wi-Fi security combination to get your clients' likes and dislikes for you to be "in-line" with them for real. It will make your unique relationships grow even faster. We live in the information era, and it is very easy to get in touch with our contacts in a gazillion ways. However, the phone will not do this for you unless you have a genius phone or Artificial Intelligence. You will have to find what your client likes all the time and download the app to find them there. Meaning, find out what makes your client happy and follow that trail. Experiencing what your client experiences with your Tank is to gather even more information. Information well filtered is knowledge and knowledge is power to achieve goals. Try to be in your clients shoes to understand a little better what their lifestyle, points of view, and demands. Also, remember that in this information era, we have to create filters and anti-virus for our protection as well. Too much garbage can also damage our hardware, be aware, you are in control and you are the smart one here.

This tool will also have applications with probes to understand the surroundings and its demands. The topography will determine the clients' wants and needs. For instance, don't sell ice to Eskimos... I do not care how big your ego is thinking you can do it. In other words, know what's hot and cold. These indications will help you fill-in the gap and stay in control in the game. If you search constantly for those gaps, then you will find many probes that will tell you today's daily news and the horoscopes in your contact list. All contacts are different and with different likes, therefore, you can also manage your contacts by group. For example, family, friend ,co-workers, etc.

These methods will allow you to use a different lingo, or a special conversation with each of your groups so the message can be delivered and remembered by all, which is the main goal. Be smart by showing your practices are smart too by keeping everything simple and accurate. Add as many contacts as you can on your Smart Phone and store them according to your plan.

It is like having a vegetable garden, you'll need to water it, give the right food, the perfect amount of water, make sure living organisms are doing their job, and light everyday so you can eat fresh too. Once you are clear how every client is carefully crafted and appreciated, sooner than you think, the tastiest veggies will be ready for reaping year after year.

Clear.

<u>Clarity = Fearless</u>

"The successful warrior is the average man, with laser-like focus". -Bruce Lee

The Stop Watch

Chapter 10

The Gold medal goes to the best athlete, no doubt about that. Most of the times to the person who did it in less time, unless you are an athlete for distance, and even so, you will be given a timed window to do the laps. Anyway, no matter what your sport of choice is, you'll need a Stop Watch. It is so useful that it is an international way to track world records. You need to have this tool very close to you and get good at timing just about everything.

When you are inside the Tank and you have locked a moving target, you only have seconds of opportunity. You have to have the Stop Watch to make all your systems and technologies be the best they can be. When we talk about technology, it is not only the hardware and updated software, it is the method of doing something better and faster than previously done.

Industries will always be evolving in ways of delivering and conducting their businesses because there is always room for improvement. The one thing that will not change is change itself. The only factor that must remain intact is the added value. Constantly search for the added value that benefits your client and your company. Systems and procedures will change, but at the end of the day, the goal is to deliver a great product on time. The stop watch will train you to observe how timing in your market takes place. It is said that "timing is everything in life", and you better believe it. Sometimes we only get one chance to swing the bat and if you are not ready, you strike out of the game.

During a lifetime, we all change forms in our body, from being a baby to growing old, with different experiences at that particular time. That's an amazing gift by the way! In addition, when you time your industry, you will know how the balloon works. Some industries you can find their pulse going up and down just like a heartbeat, and if you find the rhythm, you can hit them back like a tennis ball. Others are just plain bubbles that pop. The trick is to know the stage of these bubbles, either at the start or at the end. There will always be demands that will change the original plan of your business. When you know for sure the time is right, you can say with certainty to the rest of your warriors, it is our victory!

Everyone will see how lucky you are with the Stop Watch. Luck for me is readiness meeting opportunity. L.U.C.K also is an acronym for Living Under Correct Knowledge. It is a must to get the correct knowledge and know how to use it. Another example is like a racing team. Practicing those 5 to 10 seconds to change all four tires, fill the gas at the pit stop. Every millisecond counts. There is always a special recipe to follow otherwise it will not be successful.

As a warrior, you will need to know the importance of timing, recording, tracking, and following the recipe. Just remember the best stop watch to get is the chronological one since it is circular. Everything in our lives is circular. Like the Mayan calendar, it is cyclical therefore by definition it repeats itself. Wait attentively for your train number, it will pass sooner than later but be ready. The trick is to know if you are competing with a 12 or a 6 second pit stop.

One Mississippi.

Addition Formula : 1+1=2

"Whether I retire to bed early or late, I rise with the sun." -Thomas Jefferson

The Chivalry Flag

Chapter 11

This is 'the flag' on top of your Tank that will remind your team they are warriors. It will also remind the outside world that there you have integrity by waving your Chivalry Flag. You will be surprised how many people are looking for these positive leaders. You will find out that when your Tank represents making our neighborhoods a better place, a whole army of Tanks will appear next to yours and help you accomplish all of your missions.

It is a positive attitude carried with respect and values in and out of the Tank that works together with the mission statement. It is a reminder to all, that positive people will make calm people. This is part of the added benefit to the client, where as a result, it attracts people of the same kind. Smiles can bring enormous and beautiful peaceful crowds. Make every warrior inside your Tank be aware of such power within, by teaching them positive values and principles.

The flag will ripple positive vibrations and will send this message to everyone. It will only make your Tank stronger and wiser; giving you a greater advantage over the competition. Like for example going to a high-end coffee house. Most of us will pay a little more for a consistent product with a pleasant ambiance. Every little detail is made for positive impacts. The smell, the music, the customer service, the free Wi-Fi, everything is for the pleasure of the client, and it works! Clients will give you their honest feedback if asked correctly. Keep your real conversation light and pleasant so that you receive real feedback.

Keeping such positive mindset within your Tank, it will allow your warriors to have a more relaxed state of mind. This will allow them to perform better since you are already giving them all the tools to shine. It will be an awesome place to work, employee retention will soar, and therefore, performance will grow exponentially. Ideas will come to your office every second of the day.

Remember that all things grow with love, but you need to understand the relationship makes it last. Love is your maturity in action carried with courage and compassion. Courage is very important because it makes you an activist instead of a pacifist.

Compassion should be part of the mission statement your Tank is fueled by, and the chosen way to achieve your goals in life. It is the best shield any person can get in our universe. If it will be beneficial for everyone, therefore, you will reap that same added value.

Positive.

<u>Life formula: Relax = Peace</u>

"Talent wins games, but teamwork and intelligence wins championships." -Michael Jordan

The Key Chain

Chapter 12

This great tool needs to be close to you at all times. It is a tool to unlock a potential of wealth. The Key Chain is made of one spiral ring and many different Keys attached to the ring. Some will be small, others will be big. These Keys have different shapes and colors. Each Key opens a different door that leads to a different room. Some rooms are bigger than others, and one room is just as important as the next one.

The same way, different strings of income within a company should be in place. There should be more than one source of income for your Tank. You will have the main string of income, but you also need to offer other services or products on the back end where you make a profit. Just like the impulsive items at checkout lines, and overpriced popcorn at movie theater, etc.

I am not saying to raise your prices but measure your client needs, and offer other items or services in a timely manner. The Key Chain tool will help you remember you can fit as many keys as you want. Please do not be content with only one room and one bathroom. That is a very scarce way to live and if something happens you are out of luck, right?

You can grow and own a great apartment or later you can buy the whole building and get the penthouse view. If one room is unavailable because there was a short circuit, make sure you will have access to another room. Otherwise, you will have to stay in the same room and try to survive the smoke. Doing this will only make you weaker and your Tank will be driving on a bridge made of egg shells.

On the other hand, if you start collecting keys you will grow exponentially. Allowing your tank to move anywhere it must go by listening to your clients' demands. You can continue conquering new rooms, and it is all up to you not to be complacent. At the end of your journey, you can perfectly own all the keys to a mall if you really want.

Unlock.

Fisher Effect Equation: $MV = PT$

"Don't be afraid to go out on a limb. That's where the fruit is."- H. Jackson Browne

The Expandable Business Card

Chapter 13

"I don't have it with me..., let me check in my company car to see if have a few cards for you". Market yourself right the first time. Your information should be handy, easy to remember and easy to contact. Use all methods of contact, even if it means to advertise in a phone book. That's if your niche visit the phone book.

Consumers are brutal as they should be. The competition is also brutal just like the NFL, or tougher like Rugby. It is an intangible rough sport and your warriors need to win the championship every year. The Expandable Business Card tool will help you keep all your phones and systems ready for orders.

The system created for contacting your business should be as simple as a one, two, and three. Now days maybe to just one and two. You should not only have a business card with your contact information but also a wide range of specialties, or strengths you have within that industry.

Contacting your business should be easy so a 5 year old kid can call and a 120 year old can remember you. You must captivate your clients' subconscious with innovative experiences that creates a positive impression. Communicate with your clients in regards to what is their most comfortable and accurate way of communication. There are a number of ways to get your name out there. Here are a few to keep in mind: Website, mobile website, Google maps, QR code, VR card, Wrapped Vehicle, on the back of receipts, toys and candies with your company logo and contact information if possible, etc.

The idea is to keep things simple and catchy for clients to remember you. This way you stand out from the competition. So, the next time a client is looking for someone in your industry, you will be the first one to be remembered. Like for example Geico is green, UPS is brown, and FedEx is blue and orange. These brand stamps play a huge role inside the Tank since they give a special shopping experience to clients.

Simplifying your transaction with the client is the added value all the warriors have to create from the get go. After you have made yourself accessible, please answer the phone or make sure step two is set and ready. It is crucial to be prepared or you will be losing clients and all clients are very important.

All conversations with clients either positive or negative, they are both valuable information which in turns make you wiser for the near future demands and/or processes.

Access.

<u>Constant of a circle's circumference: $\pi = C/d$</u>

"Folks don't care what you know, til they know that you care." –Unknown

The Cookie Cutter

Chapter 14

This is an awesome tool to have in every business, unless you like to work 16 hours a day on 4 hours of sleep. Most CEO's become key personnel because nobody else knows how to do part of that work. Some keep it quiet for ego purposes, or just keep their business methods secret so they don't get fired. Resulting in out of business soon because of the burden of the sovereignty from the key personnel. Others are really smart and look for systems that will help steer those intentions of the company or goals.

The Cookie Cutter tool cuts all that drama and helps the whole Tank to move forward easily with systems in place. It is called franchising. Every business should have their own "abra-cadabra" book. This is where the magic really happens. It is the book with all top secrets of the company, ultimate of ultimate's with confidential agreements if necessary.

This tool will prove to your warriors the difference between a chef from a cook.

It is a great moment to educate and sharpen your business programs. You still need to write such a manual, even if you are not going to sell your business. You will need to measure everything. From the way the phone is answered to the way you respond to e-mails. That needs to be translated into a controlled precise outcome at all times. Record successful situations and file them appropriately.

The best entrepreneurial story is the one from Ray Crock that created McDonald's. Making it his small business and turn it into the biggest one in the whole planet. Consistency inside each franchise was the key to his success. The same thing happened to Colonel Sander's when the highway was built right on top of his restaurant, he used the Cookie Cutter tool which made him a legend.

Another positive result of franchising is that the banks will be more willing to lend you money since you are an organized and precise client that is following a Cookie Cutter tool. These are systems developed to make money on their own, managed by a simple secret recipe book.

This will allow the warrior to transfer their technician experience persona, and move full throttle into the creative or creator persona.

Replicate.

Sky is the limit formula: 10∞

"You have brains in your head. You have feet in your shoes. You can steer yourself, any direction you choose." -Dr. Seuss

The Sphere Magnet

Chapter 15

This is by far one of the sexiest WMB found in the market. It is a magnet divided in two with a North and South Pole, and it is important to understand where the poles are on the sphere. Just like it is important to know what your market likes and dislikes, as well as the likes and dislikes about your company. Tell the truth to yourself and your warriors even when it is not pretty. Once you understand that, then you can move onto step two.

Use the Sphere Magnet to attract South Pole Consumers and North Pole Consumers. Sometimes companies target every consumer the same way but the reality is that we all have different wants and needs. You will have to make sure you understand who is in one group and who is in another. You cannot just generalize all clients because they are not all equal. Once you understand this, then you will be like a movie theater playing to all audiences, and not comedy movies only.

Although, I personally think there is pleasure in variety and that is why I speak different languages, and eat different foods every day. The same goes for the business world, open opportunities and attract the right prospects. At the end of the day, your product and services have to deliver as promised, and hopefully over deliver.

This Sphere Magnet will not work if used with the wrong intentions. The added value is the convenience you gave to your clients and that is why they will continue using your services or products. It is always made for easy enchantment of the prospected client.

Also offer bundles, promotions, combos, buy one get one half off, buy two get one free. The real experience of the client will turn him or her into your spokesperson or cheerleader inside their network. That could be friends, family and co-workers. These client experiences will go far more than any ad. Trust will be anchored in your business. It will become personal from the mission statement.

Therefore, you have solidified your team of warriors and the walls of your Tank. When you have a solid word and you are frank with your clients, then they will always feel greeted sincerely, and they will come back. That is truly saying "you're welcome" without saying it.

You will have to sell the sizzle and not just banners. Once you have located the secret success for each group, then re-iterate to your clients when possible the added value once again. It is a great reminder to them because that way it will solidify the decision of the client to come back to your Tank for more. If you don't give them that extra mile you will be falling short. So line-up your clients to your ideas for a customized and organized structure.

Attractive.

Standard normal distribution: $z = (x - \mu) / \sigma$

"There is no security on the earth, there is only opportunity." -General Douglas MacArthur

The Mirror

Chapter 16

This WMB that without a doubt can catapult your Rocket Missiles and add torque to your tank at the same time. The mirror is the real-time reflection of the mentor or person you admire. Warriors need to learn from their masters, and ask them what makes them wake up at 4 o'clock in the morning. These experienced warriors are in "tune with higher frequencies" because they practice self-improvement since the moment they wake up. It is the duty of the warrior to find his or her inspiration and compare against the mirror to see if the image matches. Inspiration has to come from that gut feeling guiding the warrior.

Moreover, this presidential behavior has to come from a source of inspiration by someone. It is a choice to change in front of the mirror. It is a tool to guide you and make you aware of the world around you, to help you adapt to the situation, and then to conquer that dream persona.

The closer you are to being like your mentor, the sooner you will obtain your goals. Find a mentor or a person that is successful in your area that you would like to mimic. You should also use the internet to connect with groups involved in similar cultures. There are people like me that would like to share their experiences and help the world since we have been there and done our part. Most of us do not want others to get burned, so we can connect the dots and close the gaps where needed. The mirror will give you a reality check to take you where you need to be. If your face is dirty, then the mirror will let you know. As simple as that and without judgment. If you do not have this mirror then you will learn the hard and embarrassing way. The mentor will guide you and save you from lots of headaches, from loss of money and clients.

The Mirror is a much needed tool that needs to be taken care and polished, keeping it dirt free. The mirror should be used every day, and even sometimes you need to check it a few times during the day. Also deep clean the mirror every once in a while, unless you want to look crazy. You need to be sincerely in touch with yourself and accept the truth even when you do not look good. This brings authenticity while you are improving your skills. Keep evolving into the person you want to be but continue being who you are inside, and don't change in a weird way; like a robot. Relax and use your common sense. Rely on your values and principles.

Acquire only the best and throw away the sour experiences. This will set you apart from the norm and hopefully surpass your mentor.

Shine.

<u>Euler's Identity Equation: $ei\pi + 1 = 0$</u>

"You must be the change you wish to see in the world". -Mahatma Gandhi

The Global Positioning System

Chapter 17

Also known as G.P.S. but with a slight change of usage. When you take this tool out, you will be able to see how your Tank is in comparison to other Tanks in your industry in other parts of the world. Not just your town, think a little bit bigger. You need to be aware of how similar industries in other countries are performing their services or delivering values, and be curious on how they can relate. The Global Positioning System will guide you to check with other countries systematically on how they are evolving as opposed to your business.

Remember, industries are living organisms that change very quickly and you need to know how to time your outcome. So here is where most of the measurements take place for the equation. The domino effect is very much visible once you are on top of the wave. However, you need to think globally and understand demands to see the big picture.

It will be the tool to give you a Global Positioning to time the moon periods so you know when high or low tide is. Your tank will be visible as the center of the world and the rest your friendly neighbors will be happy to share their success and likewise. The world is a little smaller than we all think and that is the reason GPS is very important to meet your possibilities. What we do as a common unity/

community, can impact the planet immensely, and we should all be very much aware and be proactive respecting our one and only home.

This tool is also a very helpful since it gives you the arrival time, the route map, and the real-time satellite giving you directions. This will give you a great advantage over your local competition since you are finding new ways and ideas; giving you insight and creativity.

The solution you were looking for is just a few steps ahead. It is the only healthy advantage that can be added over any competitor. As a result, it will give you a sincere presentation, with power and confidence. You can say that your restaurant has the best coffee in the world and people will trust you. You are indeed the most interesting person on the planet because you have visited other places. In other words, you have to have more than just one cup of coffee to understand the product or services offered in your business.

A warrior needs to adventure to the most remote parts of the world, to try to find the perfect beans and methods performed by native cultures with traditions of more than 5,000 year old to obtain the best coffee drink in the world.

That is what I call doing your homework. This planet is our home and it is time for us to make it a better place by producing better products and services.

Travel.

Heron's Formula: S=a+b+c/2

"It is not the strongest of the species that survive, nor the most intelligent, but the one most responsive to change." -Charles Darwin

The Goody Bag

Chapter 18

Anyone successful on their own terms will tell you that first you need to give. There is no doubt that giving is where the real pleasure lies. Giving is an amazing skill to master in our lives since it is very powerful.

The abundant mentality is magical. Most people will learn it with time, hopefully. For example, let's say you are an exhibitor in a booth at a trade show giving away a bag with candy, toys, tools, clocks, etc. This is a great way for people to feel a connection and feel appreciated. By the way, your name is all over those gifts just to remind clients who got their back this time. At a trade show, you have less than 10 minutes to make a lasting impression as your prospector will meet 100 people just like you.

The more you give (intelligently), the more you get (results). So you need to appreciate your clients and those warriors within the company making that effort even when it the answer is not what you want. The good news is that there are other ways to give gifts as well. Some gifts are tangible, some others are intangible. Inspiring friends and family close to you for a while will be an abundant time of reaping all the great fruits harvested. This is where you see the added benefit at its fullest potential.

It is a positive experience that will be impacting your client for the rest of their lives, and perhaps their children as well. This is where the client will see how you are going that extra mile for them, and their family if that is the case.

Therefore, the Goody Bag should always be situated at one of the exits of your Tank. It will be wise to understand that most of these gifts should serve as advertising and that your client feels one more time how you benefited them in more ways than one.

Souvenir.

Frequency formula: $f = 1/T$

"Do or do not. There is no try".

Yoda

The Thank You Card

Chapter 19

This is the most interesting of all weapons since it becomes an inspired relationship. Saying 'Thank you' is really saying 'you are welcome'. It is that simple, and yet sometimes it is forgotten how important this piece of the puzzle really is. Showing gratitude will ignite the Knight Warrior morals that you have inside.

When you are going through a hard and difficult time, that is when you need to pull leverage by saying 'thank you '. This weight will only give you the power and the strength to carry your business forward with any other weight coming along your way, and/or to help someone else carry theirs. It is in the Thank You note that you will find the real answer to all of your questions. That is where you will find the inspiration and seal the deal. Remember inspiration means in-spirit. It is another level of forced energy and we all need to be in touch with our inspiration.

Sometimes it is harder to say than to do I am going to give you some power. When you meditate on the reaction before it happens you will be surprised how easy it is to react differently. You will never be in reaction again. It is a great skill to develop.

Thanking is an art, and it comes with practice and sincerity; the same goes with the rest of the tools in this book. It is a light torch that will be passed on to everyone you are in contact with, and it is a wave of light that will actually bounce back faster than you think.

Namaste.

Volume Formula: V= lxwxh

"Live as if you were to die tomorrow. Learn as if you were to live forever." -Mahatma Gandhi

Dedication

I am dedicating this book to all business warriors out in the field every day at the front lines of the concrete jungle; also known as the "business world". Even inside this hostile environment, amazing rewards spring from owning a business. It is a jungle but it is a balanced living organism, where you will find the sweetest and juiciest fruits, as well as the unwanted animals, insects, and terrains. It is very hard to get to your destination if you do not have the right tools to measure your steps and have the right coordinates inside the jungle.

On the other hand, when you have such tools it can become the greatest adventure of a lifetime. This book will help you get your business in shape by sharpening your own tools that you use every day. Once you start using these sharp tools subconsciously, then you can view it from the top. I made this book as simple and as short as possible, so people of all ages can make sense of their businesses, and start right leveraging their skills.

Everyone can start running a successful business now because I compacted a lot of information for small businesses, and created these metaphysical WMB so business owners can easily remember them and reuse accordingly. Any warrior can grow exponentially if they pay attention to the way they handle their actions and most importantly their thoughts. You can have the best technology but if you don't use it properly it is like not having it at all.

Like Abraham Lincoln once said: "Give me six hours to chop down a tree and I will spend the first four sharpening the axe". Your business skills need to be sharpened everyday with meditation, or else the axe will become dull, giving you literally double the work.

Thank you for taking the time to have read this book, have plenty of readiness, and welcome every second of your life because now you have new weapons in this great journey.

Enjoy!

www.ingramcontent.com/pod-product-compliance
Lightning Source LLC
Chambersburg PA
CBHW031546210526
45464CB00003B/1169